Classroom Strategies to

Classroom Strategies
to Aid the
Disabled Learner

With GLOSSARY

Jean Abbott

**Applicable to all disciplines,
academic and vocational, designed primarily for
Secondary and Middle school classroom teachers.**

Educators Publishing Service, Cambridge, Massachusetts

Library of Congress Catalog Card Number: 78-74637

ISBN: 0-8388-1674

Printed in the U.S.A.

To those teachers with whom I have had the privilege to work,
and who have given so generously of their time to their students
and to me, and to all other teachers who are concerned about students.

Contents

Preface ix

1 What's It All About — Some Generalizations 1

2 Important Things You Should Know 5

3 Distortions 7

4 Learning Styles of Students with Learning Disabilities 19

5 Meeting Your Learning Disabled Student 23

6 Classroom Strategies 25

7 The New Federal Legislation — How It Helps *You* 43

8 The New Federal Legislation — Not to Panic 47

Glossary 51

PREFACE

Repeatedly and with increasing frequency, secondary school teachers are expressing their concerns about teaching the disabled learners in their classrooms. Who will these students be? What will they be like? What to expect? What materials to use? In addition, the increasing use of technical language by learning disabilities specialists introduces to many teachers a vocabulary both unique and mystifying. This further compounds the problem for classroom teachers who are asked to meet the disabled students' "special needs" and at the same time carry on with the other twenty-eight to thirty-two members of the class.

For these teachers, the dilemma is real.

It is also intensified with recent passage of State and Federal legislation for the "special needs" child.

Most of the literature on learning disabilities focus on a) recognition, diagnosis and testing, b) working with the learning disabled student in a small group tutorial situation and/or c) working with the learning disabled student in a self-contained elementary classroom situation. Very little of the available literature is addressed to the secondary or middle school classroom teacher, who has imposed upon him or her the additional handicap of having his or her students for only one period during the school day.

The situation is further complicated and exacerbated by the fact that, except to the medical profession, the entire area of learning disabilities is relatively new, about fifteen or twenty years. Hence, teachers who received their degrees some years ago start out at a disadvantage. Even though they may have had years of successful teaching experience in dealing with learning disabled students, the new and unfamiliar terminology makes them feel uneasy and unprepared.

It is to meet the needs of these secondary and middle school teachers, needs expressed, unacknowledged or subliminal, that this book has been undertaken.

The purpose is two-fold. The primary thrust is to provide some specific classroom strategies. These suggestions and strategies are:

- designed for the *classroom teacher*
- intended for use with disabled learners *in the classroom*
- geared for *secondary and middle school classes*
- usable within *any discipline*

The second purpose is to remove the mystery that seems to surround the field of learning disabilities and its terminology: to remove the veil and to reveal, through examples, what is meant by the various technical terms. In addition, a glossary is provided at the end of the text.

As every field has come to develop its own vocabulary, and to refine it as more knowledge becomes available, so too has the terminology of learning disabilities developed. In the last fifteen to twenty years the field has expanded rapidly. It has now reached the point where the classroom teacher's main concern may well have become the verbiage rather than the learner, the student. The hope is to reverse this trend of mis-ordered priorities by providing classroom teachers with a working tool, one which "translates" the verbiage into everyday, working English.

As for the classroom strategies, although they may also be used in elementary classrooms, they are designed especially for the secondary and middle school teacher, for whom very little practical material is available. The emphasis and most of the material for the learning disabled child is geared for the elementary level, which is as it should be. However, even when this is the case, not all learning disabled students are able to develop adequate compensating mechanisms for their handicap. Thus, they, as well as others, are still trying to cope as they move on through the school system. Indirectly, then, this is also a book for students as well as for teachers since, in the last analysis, it is our students who count.

Finally, I would not have had the temerity to undertake this subject if it were not for the help and advice so freely offered over the years by my colleagues including those whose expertise in the area of learning disabilities has been invaluable. To them and to the many other teachers who have been and continue to be so generous with their time, to me as well as to their students, my most heartfelt and greatful thanks.

It is hoped that what follows will prove helpful as well as to allay any anxieties that may exist.

X

Classroom Strategies to Aid the Disabled Learner

1

WHAT'S IT ALL ABOUT — SOME GENERALIZATIONS

Students with learning disabilities are neither monsters nor barbarians. Nor are they imbeciles. In most cases their IQ's are well within the normal, average range, sometimes even above average. Don't make the mistake of being misled by what is indicated from the SAT scores on the back of the Cumulative Record Card. The trick here is to remember that SAT's reflect a *timed* test, assume an average ability to mainipulate a test booklet, pencil, and a computerized, space-age answer sheet. These are all assumptions made about the testee. Furthermore, they are made *before* anyone even begins to consider his ability to read, and to follow written directions. All this can greatly affect his ability to read and to process the material inherent in the questions themselves. (Remember your own GRE? Your Miller Analogies?)

The learning disabled student is not stupid. If you *ask him* the question he can probably tell you the answer. If you insist on a written test he may surprise you with his knowledge, *provided* you can bring yourself to be flexible enough to give him more time, or to allow him to take the test orally.

Sound familiar?

Of course. You've had students like this before. Their grades weren't all that red hot and you had to gear up your Ingenuity Department in order to come up with some different strategies that would enable them to learn.

You will probably also recall that what worked so well for Joe didn't work very well at all for Paul. Why? Because there are varieties of learning disabilities. Thus, Joe's may have been in the visual area (he had trouble reading) whereas Paul's was in the hearing area (he couldn't sort out the words of your lecture fast enough for them to have meaning for him.)

Both are manifestations of learning disabilities. However, each is quite different. Thus, the same prescription will not work for all. In the same manner, a prescription for the common cold is not going to do you much good if it's a toothache that's killing you. Or filling up the gas tank of your car isn't going to make it go if the trouble is a dead battery.

In short, different strategies are necessary for different kinds of learning problems. Thus, in order to make these strategies more meaningful, it is necessary first to be familiar with the difficulties under which the learning disabled learner labors, so that his time in your class will be meaningfully spent. There is also an indirect benefit to you as a teacher as you observe him becoming engaged in learning in your class.

Remember, you *have* had these students before. It's just that before they did not arrive packaged and labelled. Thus, you will probably recognize some of the strategies and, quite possibly, have invented others yourself that haven't been included.

Students with learning disabilities constitute between two and ten percent of our school population, with some estimates as high as twelve percent. In the past, with rigid curricula and inflexible teachers, many of these students dropped out in their early high school years, sometimes even prior to that time. Many still do. Thus, once again, allay your apprehensions. You have already met these students, perhaps not many but certainly some. They were your pluggers. Most are not discipline problems and, when this is the case, it is more a matter of frustration-with-self than an outright conscientious effort to sabotage your class or to give you, personally, a bad time. It is a good point to keep in mind.

In essence, the secret of success in working with learning disabled students is in the teacher's attitude. Always remember that the student has probably had a terrible time in school, frequently as far back as the first grade. He can't perform, or he can't perform on a par with his peers. Therefore, he thinks he is stupid. By the time that he reaches the middle school, he is thoroughly convinced that he is stupid. No matter how much you point out that he has difficulty yes, but that he is NOT stupid, he will not believe you. As high school looms closer he may become very depressed. Talk of suicide is not uncommon. He may be the best ball player or the best fixer of bikes and/or cars and motors but to him this counts for nothing. "I'm stupid!" Thus, for the learning disabled student of any age, the most important thing is his teacher's attitude toward him. He needs your faith desperately.

Not only does he labor under his learning difficulty but he also labors under the self-imposed hurdles of "I'm stupid" or "I'm dumb" which have become more and more firmly entrenched with the passage of time. He needs teachers who care. Not just a lip-service caring, with quick reference to grade book. Real caring.

If you say that you will help him after school, BE THERE! If you let yourself get delayed by coffee or colleagues, or even your principal or superintendent, you'll let him down. It may translate to him that you are just *saying* that you care when you really don't at all. It will also reinforce his own feeling of unworthiness — that he's stupid and doesn't matter.

In the same vein, if you offer to give him an untimed test, do it. And make your arrangements with him privately. Avoid making a big deal about it and embarrassing him in front of the class.

If you offer him the choice of putting his report on tape or cassette, be sure his "report" is graded and handed back at the same time as is everyone else's. Incidentally, maybe other students would also be interested in doing their report on cassette, too. This would be good as it makes your disabled student less "different", more like the other students, nothing special about him.

Incidentally, each of these last two varieties is a form of individualized instruction. Individualized instruction does *not* mean a separate curriculum for each student that you have. It means adjustments of assigned tasks.

The beginning of the school year is the time when situations in which you may unwittingly let your learning disabled student down are most apt to arise. Not enough time has yet elapsed for you to ascertain the strengths and weaknesses of your students. Therefore, should you inadvertently call on one of them during the mutual get-to-know-you period, try not to be too put off if he gives you an "I don't know" answer. Stay cool. You usually do anyway. Before you come around to him with another verbal question try him (and the class, of course) on a written quiz. Is he purposefully giving you a bad time, or is it that he really has difficulty responding in an oral situation?

Instead of "I don't know" you may get a flip remark — or both together. Don't let yourself fall into his trap. Even though it may be the last class of the day and you are tired. Don't let yourself fall for this old chestnut. The intent behind these words indeed is to have you become exasperated, get on your high horse, and send him out of the room. (Anything is perferable to letting you see how "dumb" he is, and of having his peers ridicule him.) Recognize this tactic for what it is — his defense for his incapability, because of his learning problems, to respond intelligently to what you have asked. (If you were lecturing it may be that his hearing channel may be impaired in such a way that he needs more time to assimilate what he hears before he is able to respond. In other words, he needs more time to "transcribe/translate" what he hears into what he says, to switch from his words-that-he-hears channel to words-that-he-says channel.) Refuse to allow yourself to get side-tracked by his behavior. Zero in on the cause, not the effect.

Or was everyone reading the same paragraph and then you asked questions? Perhaps he reads very slowly and wasn't able to finish the paragraph in the time allotted.

Whereas "I don't know" may be acceptable for the present, flippancy or rudeness is not to be tolerated at any time. What to do? If he gets away

3

with it this time the whole class could become troublesome.

One solution is to tell him, CALMLY, that you would like to see him for just a few minutes after the class is over. This makes it clear to both him and to the rest of the class that such behavior is not going to be tolerated by you. It also has the added advantage of giving you a private moment with him. Then, when you are talking with him after class, *ask* him about his previous school experience. Has school been hard for him? Has he had tutoring somewhere along the line? Does he find it difficult to follow spoken presentations, written presentations, reading in class? Has he discovered any methods, techniques and/or strategies that make it easier for him to learn? Listen to what he says. Respect his sense of self.

He will probably be so knocked out by the unexpectedness of your obvious concern, that your potential discipline problem will evaporate into thin air; *provided* of course, that you also respect his confidences, and are sincere in your efforts to act on what he has told you. You've long known that not all students have the same learning style, learn at the same rate, etc. Now you've just gotten some first-hand "hard data" on one of them. From a teen-ager, that's quite a compliment!

2

IMPORTANT THINGS YOU SHOULD KNOW

The fact that the student with learning difficulties has been referred to as "he" is no accident. For some reason, there are many more learning disabled boys than girls. Authorities vary, citing figures of six out of ten, seven out of ten, to even eight out of ten.

Together with the "why" of learning disabilities itself, the male/female ratio of learning disabled students still goes without a scientifically definitive explanation. A minority continue to adhere to the theory (to date not yet unequivocally demonstrated) that there is some biological defect. The majority lean toward a "short-circuit" theory. This is not, repeat NOT, a brain damage theory. Rather, it recognizes that all necessary components and elements for learning and functioning are present; that within this intricate complex/network a connection has failed to form/function along one, or sometimes more than one channel. If the "short-circuit" is within the learning-by-seeing pathway, the student's disability will be in the visual area. THIS DOES NOT MEAN THAT HIS SIGHT IS IMPAIRED. NOR DOES IT MEAN THAT HE NEEDS OR SHOULD WEAR GLASSES. It *does* mean that the information and sensations that his brain receives through his eyes are, in some way distorted. The distortions can manifest themselves in several different ways. (Some examples of distortions are given in the following chapter.)

The same is true of hearing. It is not that the student cannot distinguish what he hears or has a hearing loss. It is that there is an impairment, a "short-circuit" in one or more of the areas involved in clear aural reception. As with vision, the distortions can manifest themselves in a variety of ways. Examples of these are also given in the following chapter.

Thus the fact remains that to date the specific cause or causes of learning disabilities have yet to be definitively determined.

In point of fact, outside of the medical field, it is only within the last fifteen or twenty years that learning disabilities per se have been recognized. Current definitions refer to "disorders" and/or "delayed development" in the aforementioned processes involved for effective use of language expression, (written and oral,) with concomitant difficulties/impairments in the listening, thinking, speaking, reading, writing, spelling and/or math areas.

A learning disability has also been referred to as the "hidden handicap" since some teachers mistake the student's inability to achieve/progress as a result of "not trying", inattentiveness, short attention span, etc. They stop short instead of having second thoughts and looking beyond these symptoms.

Currently there is agreement among authorities that there is no cure for the learning disability. Thus, in the absence of a cure the learning disabled student must learn to cope by using alternative strategies. He must develop compensating mechanisms. In other words, he must develop alternative methods/strategies in order to learn. Unlike the student with the broken leg, his disability will not go away with time. Rather, his faulty circuits will not repair themselves no matter how much time and attention they receive. Instead, he will have to continue to compensate and to cope for the rest of his life. Perhaps the miracle is that in most instances he not only can but does.

3

DISTORTIONS

An understanding of the way in which the learning disabled child's handicap interferes with your instruction is vital.

Unfortunately, many teachers tend to equate learning disabled children with "slow learners." This is a very grave error and does a dis-service to both.

The "slow learner" is, by definition, *slow*. His perceptions are clear, and all sensory channels are GO. *He does not have any short-circuits*. Hence, he has no distortions in perception. He just needs more time. He is *slow*.

On the contrary, the learning disabled child is *disabled*. He is handicapped! Input which comes to him through his short-circuited channels gets distorted en route and arrives in varying degrees of distortion. Thus, his handicap requires *adjustment of input* so that the input will travel along his intact circuits. (Adjustments are usually necessary for output as well.) In other words, his handicap requires adjustments/variations in the ways in which material is presented to him (and also desired feedback or output.)

It is not just a condition which "more time" will cure. It is a very real handicap, in every sense of the word.

More time may be needed also, but unless adjustments are made to input and/or expected output little if any progress in learning will be made.

Chapter 6 is devoted exclusively to specific strategies and suggestions for varying input and output for learning disabled students.

However, before proceeding to these strategies themselves, let us first take a look at some examples and illustrations of some of the varieties in which these distortions can manifest themselves. They may be Visual Distortions (the student who learns best through what he hears), Auditory Distortions (the student who learns best through what he sees), and/or Processing Distortions including sequencing and memory.

VISUAL DISTORTIONS

Therefore, The Auditory Learner

One of the distortions most commonly referred to and most easily recognized is "reversals." The student "reverses" letters, most commonly b and d, w and m, p and g. He reverses them because he can't "discriminate" between them. In other words, he can't "see," literally, the difference. He may read "saw" for "was", "sag" for "sad", "now" for "how", "ban" for "pan", "tan" for "fan", etc. To get an idea of the difficulty that this poses for him, try reading the following selection.

> Today I was Jim. He saw over by the dridge that is near my house. His god saw with him. His god is sometimes dab. For instance, today he had a piece of dreab that he had stolen. Another time he tore a gape from my book. *

Think how you would feel if you were called on to read this orally. And how much worse it would be if you had to read it in front of the whole class!

Now answer the following questions; before looking below to the "translation."

1. Where did he see Jim?
2. Why is Jim's dog bad?
3. What did Jim's dog do today?

---

* TRANSLATION:

> Today I saw Jim. He was over by the bridge that is near my house. His dog was with him. His dog is sometimes bad. For instance, today he had a piece of bread that he had stolen. Another time he tore a page from my book.

To simulate the horror of a spelling test pick a dozen words from a foreign language with which you are totally unfamiliar. Give yourself a night to learn them for tomorrow's quiz. Remember that this is not just a one-shot thing but a task that will continue for 180 days.

Try some math when you aren't really sure if it's a $+$ for adding, a x for multiplying, a $-$ for subtracting or a $\div$ for dividing. Think of the numbers themselves. For instance, 254 plus 33 $=$ may look like 452 plus 33 $=$. (How lucky that the second number has two of the same thing!)

As regards math, 24 $\div$ by 6 may be seen as 6 $\div$ by 24. In the same matter, 75 $-$ 50 may be seen as 50 $-$ 75.

This is also the student who has a difficult time finding his way about the building. He is confused by direction.

In addition to reversals, sometimes all of the letters appear to be the same height. Try this by yourself and then with a group of your friends or fellow teachers. Notice how it is even more difficult to "translate" when there are other conversations going on in the room, or with TV or a radio in the background.

> I he first woman in the United States to quality for a pilot's license was Kuth Quimby. At the time she was a newspaper woman, working in Boston.
> After qualifying for her license, her next determination was to be the first woman to fly across the English Channel. It had been done by a man in 1909. In this she succeeded.
> Tragically, in 1912, she was killed while flying in an air show over Boston.

Were you able to finish in the time allotted? Ready for the questions?

1. What is the name of the first woman in the United States to obtain a pilot's license?
2. What was her occupation at the time?
3. Had anyone flown the English Channel before her?
4. Etc., etc., etc.

Occasionally the distortion is a matter of the lines not being straight. They may travel up and down as they flow across the page. You've seen this yourself, no doubt, with hastily made xerox or ditto copies. Remember how annoying it can be. For instance:

The first Women's Air Race was held in August of 1929.

The course was from Santa Monica, California to Cleveland, Ohio. Twenty women entered. Among them were Amelia Earhart

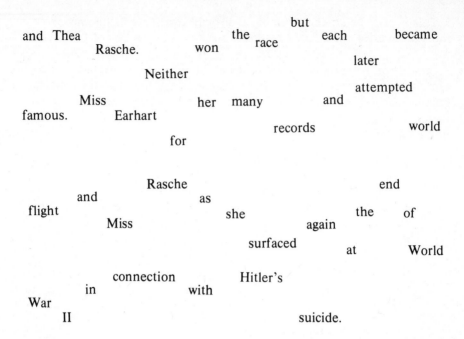

and Thea Rasche. Neither won the race but each became later
Miss Earhart her many and attempted famous. records world
for

Rasche and as end
flight Miss she again the of
surfaced at World

connection Hitler's
in with
War
II suicide.

What would it feel like if everything you read did this? Would you still read the newspaper every night? How about looking up the sources for the paper you have to research and write for the evening course you're taking to insure that salary step increment.

Not distortion, but equally frustrating for students, are problems with skipping lines and/or words, or difficulty being able to keep their place in the book, map, chart or whatever.

In the last example the student could at least perceive the words. He could also perceive the spaces in between the words. Thus, at least he had the words in their entirety. Not all students do. They are not able to distinguish — discriminate — these spaces between the words. Thus, they incline to breaking the letters into words at random places. Try this:

NewMe xicoh ashad avari edhis tory. It'sbe ginni ngswe reind ian.Th epueb lovil lages along theRi oGran deand thera iding Nava jofro mtheW est.
Thefi rstco nquere rswer etheS panis h.The ycame upfro mthes outh, fromM exic o.Itw asave rylar geforc ewith Mexic ansdr aftedb ytheS pani shha vingto domuc hofth ework.

Late rcame thetr ader salon gtheS anteF eTrai l,and later still theUS Army.

Atone point aConf edera teFor ceatt empte dtoin vadeN ewMexi cobut wasdr ivenb ack.

Thust oday,S anteF eisan amalg amof ourci viliz ation s.TheI ndian, Mexic an,Spa nish, andAm erica n,thel atter himse lfana malga m.

It looks like a coded message, doesn't it? Sometimes reading aloud can ease this confusion. Notice how much longer it takes to read this way.

Remember too, it isn't just the reading alone that's required. The student must *do* something about what he has read. "List in order of their appearance the people of New Mexico." "Who were the original occupants?" "Does the selection tell you why they came?" (How much, really, do you remember after fighting your way through this paragraph?)

What if this was just one paragraph of several pages which will be covered in tomorrow's quiz.

Finally, imagine the student who "sees" all printed matter as its mirror image. He may have trouble with directionality, inclining to read everything from right to left, as in Arabic, rather than from left to right.

Try this for a real handicap:

I awoke this morning to the news of a tragedy. A traffic reporting helicopter had crashed into an apartment building located near one of the main arteries into the city. It exploded
on impact. Fire broke out almost immediately. There is a
question as to whether or not the regular reporter or a substi-
tute was aboard. The pilot's name was not given, only that
he had radioed just prior to the crash that he was about to
make an emergency landing. Men from the news media are
rushing to the scene, reporting from their cars that it is a
three alarm fire, the number of injured still unknown, and
the nearest hospital already on a "Red Alert."

Were you able to read in the time allotted? Now answer the following questions?

1. Where did the helicopter crash?
2. Was the regular reporter on board?
3. How bad is the fire?
4. Where are current reports coming from?

Do you think you might have been more successful if you had had to read only half of the paragraph?

All in all, heavy going! The wonder is that the student with visual learning problems has stuck it out this far! The fact that he is still in school is a tribute and a credit to his family and his former teachers.

He needs to get his information through his ears, his auditory channel. He is an "aural" learner.

Specific suggestions and strategies for helping this student who learns through his ears are given in the chapter on Classroom Strategies.

AUDITORY DISTORTIONS

Therefore, the Visual Learner

One of the most common distortions experienced by the student with an auditory difficulty is that of distinguishing between sounds, of "discriminating" between sounds. This is more than just a matter of distinguishing nuances of sound; it is that he has trouble distinguishing between the sounds themselves. For instance, between "bat" and "bad".

It's a bit like listening to a foreign language that you don't understand too well. You can pick out the "hello" and "goodby" and some Americanized words like "le weekend" that you may get because you know them through a different context. However, in point of fact you have to admit that you have only a very hazy idea if any of what the conversation is about. All those unfamiliar words sound just like one big long one. In truth, you really haven't been able to tell where one word ends and the next one begins. It is just one big slurr.

Now imagine answering questions based on this conversation.

Another fairly common handicap is that of background noise (such as other students moving about the classroom, a group at work at one side of the room, the student next to him shuffling through his papers, tapping his pencil, drumming his fingers, etc.) In some cases the disabled student is not able to "tune out" this background noise, and it goofs up what he is trying to hear and understand.

To simulate the experience, tune your transistor radio to a talk show, then put it near your ear. Now listen to what the person across the room is explaining to you, about the different characters in a short story, about the advantages and disadvantages of buying a hand calculator with a floating decimal, about the latest price increases for coffee, or the distinction between fusion and fission.

Were you able to understand the explanations? Do you now have a basis for judgement? How about explaining it to a friend, to someone else, to the whole class!

12

Another kind of hearing distortion is static, just like the static which you sometimes get on the radio including a "white out", a space without noise, as when you go under a bridge.

The student can hear you but instead of receiving an even flow from you he gets it in broken up pieces. The static is such that it may even break up words, so that what he hears is a series of nonsense syllables. Maybe he catches a word here and there, but it is all pretty disconnected.

Actually, the sensation is similar to listening to your radio when there is static. It comes through broken and garbled and is most frustrating, particularly if you are listening to the news and a great flood or other disaster has taken place in the world. You go crazy trying to find out where it is, already worrying about kith and kin.

So it is with the static-interference student. He doesn't know whether you are in mid-sentence, the next sentence, or into the one after that. He breathes when you pause at the end of your paragraph. He still doesn't know whether Rome destroyed the world or was itself destroyed.

The game is easy to play. Try listening to a friend while they're unloading a truck just outside. Or asking directions when you're down in the subway, with trains clattering in and out all the time. Did you understand the directions? How well would you have been able to carry on a conversation with a friend?

Bear in mind that if you ask to have something repeated you run the risk of your "teacher's" impatience and the possibility of incurring some form of punishment. On the other hand, if you don't respond at all you run the same risk and may get an "F" for the day.

Not a very fun game, is it.

PROCESSING DISTORTIONS

Including Sequencing and Memory

Not so much a distortion per se but equally inhibiting for the school learner are disabilities which affect a student's "processing."

"Processing" refers to his ability to examine, assess, remember, winnow, integrate and internalize information received, *input.* In short, to learn. Implied also is the ability to assimilate and recall, *output.* In a school situation it is further implicit that this output, (this ability to recall), be demonstrated, either orally or in writing and, (the catch), within normal time limits.

Thus, his processing center is his refinery, if you will. The raw material (input) is received, is acted upon, and emerges in the form of a marketable commodity (output). In a school situation it is this output that becomes the marketable commodity that teachers require. This is as opposed to rote learning. Rote material can be fed back, it can even be remarketed, but very seldom has it been subjected to much, if any, refining. This is not to say that rote learning is a bad thing. It isn't. But some of what is learned by rote should, sooner or later, be subjected to some scrutiny. In addition, it needs to be assimilated for its usefulness as a cornerstone and building block. In short, it needs to be "processed."

Fortunately, in many instances where processing is a problem, only one channel is affected. Thus, information can be processed/refined if it is "beamed in" through a different channel.

For instance, the student may not have any difficulty processing the steps necessary to taking apart and rebuilding a lawn mower engine from the diagram supplied. He may also be able to process what he hears and hence be able to do the same task from oral directions. However, he has a terrible time processing what he sees. Give him a set of written directions and he is in trouble.

An integral part of processing is sequencing and memory.

Sequencing is knowing the order in which things happen, of which things come first, in other words, of having one's ducks in order.

Imagine if you weren't sure whether Friday came after Wednesday or Monday. What a mess your social calendar would be in! How difficult to plan what you were going to do tomorrow when you're not sure exactly which day of the week tomorrow is. Or to tell time; or the months of the year. How to plan intelligently for those tax bills, to say nothing of meetings!

These are the students who frequently get their daily class schedules mixed up and who get really confused when, because of an assembly, the periods within the school day are switched around. They forget appointments and get confused as to whether band or football practice is today or tomorrow.

They may also have difficulty internalizing time as well. Their time sense is off, resulting in the difficulty of internalizing whether one or three hours have elapsed.

Some students can tell you all about the War Between the States but they won't be able to tell you whether the Battle of Gettysburg was before or after Sherman's March through Georgia. They will have a terrible time in a science class and probably drive you to distraction! Despite your demonstration they may not be able to remember whether the second liquid is added to the first before or after heating. If you're lucky the visual learner may be able to sequence all right if he *sees* you do it, and does it with your help, and the auditory learner if he *hears* you describe it. Thus, BE SURE THAT YOU HAVE HIS ATTENTION, whichever channel is indicated. Sit him right down in front of you. Be sure that he is LOOKING AT YOU ALL THE TIME! Have him verbalize the steps as you do them, then review them for him.

For the student whose sequencing is impaired learning his multiplication tables is well nigh impossible. Since his sense of the progression of things is mal-functioning the concept of multiplication tables holds little meaning for him.

The student who reverses his letters (b for d, etc.) is exhibiting the same deficiency.

Once again, the need to know the student's learning style, his most efficient memory channel, is of the utmost importance.

Memory and sequencing are closely intertwined. Memory functions most efficiently when that which must be remembered is organized in sequence.

Some students may demonstrate poor memory in a classroom situation but exhibit a perfectly OK memory in their after school jobs. This is partly because DOING aids memory best. (It is one reason why vocational schools have such a high success rate. Other reasons are because their teaching is in all of the three learning modes, visual, auditory and motor.)

Some students manage fairly well with short term memory but have difficulty retaining information over a long term basis.

Some students remember more than you might suppose if they are judged solely on output. For them the difficulty is information retrieval, rather than memory alone.

Still other students may not be able to recall information but are able to recognize it in its printed form, perhaps even in its cursive, your handwriting, form.

Processing may also affect the student's facility with writing, his "fine motor" coordination. It is possible that it is physically difficult for him to write. Thus, where this is the case, it may take him much longer to bring forth his marketable commodity, the output which you require.

He will also be at a further disadvantage where copying from the board and/or note taking are required.

Another example of a processing problem is that of having to switch channels within the processing center. In other words, from receiving input via one channel (seeing) to having to provide output via a different channel (oral). This is known as "crossing modalities."

For instance, if input and requested output are both oral then he is OK (unless recall is a problem). However, if input is aural and requested output is to be written then he may be in trouble. However, this is harder than aural-oral since "written" can take many forms. It can be words, maps, diagrams, charts, etc.

In the same manner, for another student, if input is visual and requested output is written the chances are pretty good that he will be able to do it. However, like his counterpart, if input is visual and requested output is oral he may experience great difficulty.

Sometimes the student may know it in his head but he just can't get it out. Sort of like stuttering, a mental stuttering. Remember the times when you knew it but you just couldn't say it, or you couldn't recall the right word, or remember someone's name? For you a minor irritation and embarrassment at the time. But imagine how annoying and frustrating this would be if it happened to you for half of your waking day! What a horror to sit in class knowing that you may be called on at any moment.

Less obvious is still another form of processing difficulty, that of the "delayed response." On the surface it may appear as if the student is recalcitrant when it comes to classroom participation. Actually, it is that he needs more time to assimilate — to process — input, as well as to formulate — to process — his reply. As a result he is not ready with the answer when called upon to reply or to write it and may even be still thinking about it as you move on to the next aspect. Try not to mistake this for daydreaming. It is easy to interpret this as a student who spends his time in class tuning in, then tuning out.

Basic to the difficulties inherent in a processing problem is the fact that if/when the input comes in distorted, the error may frequently be compounded at the "refinery." For this student, input via his functioning channel is vital! If his best channel is visual provide all the visual clues/cues that you can. If he has difficulty processing aural input be sure to speak slowly, clearly and distinctly, and try to keep the vocabulary simple.

Finally, input that travels freely, and has not been blocked or impeded in the refinery may suddenly seem not to make sense any more. This can happen due to subsequent input that comes in via a faulty channel and/or hits that part of the processing schema that distorts. What he thought he understood/knew now seems contradicted, due to the distorted and hence *mis*-information that has gotten through. Thus, the student is thrown back once again. Which is right? He must go back and recheck his source.

Many disabled students, particularly those with temporal and sequencing problems, have a terrible day when school principals decide to switch the class schedule around, such as when, because of an assembly, the first and last periods of the day are transposed. The students get confused. He gets off to a bad day's start by the last-period-being-the-first switch, and is apt to remain confused for the rest of the day. Sometimes he goes to lunch at the wrong time and then winds up "in trouble" for having "cut" a class.

16

Students with learning difficulties also have a much harder time adjusting to schools with "rotating" class schedules, schedules in which each subject comes at a different time each day.

For the disabled student, a change, any change, in routine is a threat. It is even more the case if the change is sudden.

Whether channels are intact or impaired, it is, in the last analysis, within the processing center that internalization takes place. Thus, for the student with channels impaired the task is not easy. When he has been able to strengthen his areas of weakness and develop alternative strategies he has made a major breakthrough. Ultimately, all learning depends upon successful processing.

4

LEARNING STYLES
OF STUDENTS WITH LEARNING DISABILITIES

A great deal is made in Educational Circles of "The Learning Process." Unfortunately, this seems to have come to mean the *process of CURRICULUM progression*. What has been lost in this assimilation is the original intent, that of the *learning process of the CHILD.* The process of his individual "learning style."

The "learning style" for most children includes input via auditory, visual and motor channels, as is apparent from the preceding chapter. In other words, they learn through their eyes and through their ears and through their muscles (touching, talking, writing, etc. Doing.) Also most children will learn better/faster/more easily through one of these modes/ channels/pathways than they will through the other. You probably do yourself. Most people do. You've heard people say "If I have time to say it out loud to myself first, then I can really remember!" Or "If I can just see it, I can remember it so much better!" Or "If I do it, I remember it best."

Everyone has a learning style that works best for him or her. The learning disabled student is no different. Like his peers the preferred process is either visual or auditory or motor, or any combination (some have difficulty with two or more modes.)

However, whereas his peers have their less-favored mode, one or more modes of the learning disabled student is mal-functioning. In terms of school learning, it sometimes seems as if it would be better if it were out of order all together. Thus, instead of a no-signal-at-all through this mode, the learning disabled student is beset with a signal that may bring him erroneous data.

For the child with visual problems it may be as if he is looking at/ seeing/being shown a "w" but the message/signal that he gets is an "m", as discussed in the chapter on distortions.

Thus, whereas learning styles for most students can be described fairly simply, for the disabled student they will need to be considerably expanded and very carefully stated. Again, from the earlier discussion of distortions, the importance of knowing your student's learning style should be obvious.

Specifically, there are numerous variations within the domain of visual learning disabilities. Thus, there are numerous possible variations on the kind and extent of the disability, and hence the learning style, especially if sequencing, memory, etc. are also affected. There will probably be some elements common to all but no two learning styles will be entirely the same. Again, there will be similarities, but no two will be entirely similar.

For instance, a student who learns best visually may not, in all cases, be able to read easily and/or well. Reading is just one of the forms which visual input can take (others are maps, charts, drawings, acting, movies, TV, observing others, doing it himself, etc.) Thus, although his learning style is visual, further amplification is necessary when describing this in order to point out how well and how best he reads.

Similarly, the student who learns best through his auditory channel may not be able to repeat everything right back. He can listen and understand, but he may have trouble repeating it. Or, he can repeat it for you but he hasn't internalized very much. Thus, again, the learning style needs to be expanded.

The same is true for other varieties of learning difficulties.

In all instances of diagnosed learning disability there will have been testing. In all likelihood the testing will have been done by a teacher who has specialized in working with learning disabled students. If you are not able to locate either the testing report, or a report summarizing the initial learning disability testing, by all means seek out the learning disabilities teacher for a consultation.

Your student's Special Needs teacher or tutor may not have his learning style down pat during the first days of school but she certainly will within the first week or two. Further, she can help you with interpreting the special learning disability testing results, should you be rusty on current terminology or the test an unfamiliar one. She can also be very helpful should the write-up not be available for some reason.

In fact, the sooner you hook up with your student's tutor the better for all three of you. Each of you represents a part of the whole. It's a bit like an isosoles triangle; the student at the apex, and you and his Special Needs teacher or tutor providing strong base supports, doing your best to hold your respective angles so that the sides won't waver and your student fall ignomineously to the ground.

Each has a part to play.

Your part is to work with him to increase his knowledge.

In order to do this to the best of your ability you need to know HOW he learns, his learning style.

His learning disabilities Special Needs teacher or tutor is concentrating on teaching him different ways to learn, emphasizing the use of functioning channels and the development of better functioning of his weak channels. She is providing him with different tools (techniques as well as devices) for learning to learn and thus to be able to be successful in your classroom.

The advantage of consulting with his Special Needs teacher or tutor is obvious. She is trying to provide your student with a bag of tricks (strategies) which will help him with his learning in the classroom. Naturally the sensible thing for the classroom teacher to do is to find out what these techniques are and capitalize on them.

Getting together with your students Special Needs teacher or tutor has the added advantage of helping the student too. For him it is additional reinforcement. First because he is being asked to do the same thing in some (one would like to think all) classes; this immediately reduces some of his anxiety and frees up that energy. Second, it serves to reinforce his alternative (and frequently more time consuming) methods of learning. Third, the more that things follow the same pattern, the easier life is for him and stress is reduced. The less stress he is under, the more energy he has for learning.

In other words, the fewer the variables, the more successful he is apt to be. Remember too, success in school is something with which he has not had too much experience. Therefore, utilize his strengths. Build on his strengths.

As for the apex, the student, you will find that ninety-five percent of the time, with the kind of help just described, he will do his part.

Unfortunately, many classroom teachers fall into the error of expecting his Special Needs teacher or tutor to do it all. (These are usually the "purveyors of information" people, not Teachers.) Not only is this unjust but it is unrealistic. In addition, it points out the lack of understanding and comprehension of the differences between the two positions.

The classroom teacher's responsibility is the infusion of knowledge into her students — the expression of concepts, the exchange of ideas. All of this in a classroom which comprises between 25-35 students, no mean feat! Nevertheless, the more attuned she is to the various learning styles in general, and to the particular learning styles of her learning disabled students, the more successful they both will be.

On the other hand, the responsibility of the Special Needs teacher is to provide the student with alternative, compensating learning techniques; with ways to learn to learn. This includes providing a well-structured program of instructions to assist him in lessening the gap between what he has learned to do and what he still must learn. Since the variables within a given learning disability are many, this can only take place successfully with small groups of students at a time.

In short, the difference is one of *emphasis*. For the classroom teacher, CONTENT: for the Special Needs teacher, PROCESS.

The tragedy is that sometimes classroom teachers lose their balance. They become so heavily weighted in their emphasis on *content* that *process* suffers. (As do they and their students as the year progresses.)

In the last analysis, when the years of high school are over, many of the facts will have been forgotten. However, if the job has been done well then all may relax, knowing that process remains, and that LEARNING will be on-going.

5

MEETING YOUR LEARNING DISABLED STUDENT

As your students come into your classroom and take their seats you will observe, of course, several behaviors. Probably these will range from the quiet, polite, friendly students to the somewhat flip, and noisy, and the swaggerer. Notice too where they choose to sit, whether they look at you and whether or not they are willing to make eye contact. Note too which, if any, seem overly nervous and/or tense.

It is the nervous and tense of whom you need to be particularly aware. The chances are that these are your disabled students, and let us hope that there are only one or two per class.

Try to keep them within your peripheral vision. Operate on the theory that they are disabled until you have had a chance to establish otherwise. Avoid situations which will require your having to call on them (such as calling on "every third person" or "every other row" or whatever. Furthermore, if work is to be done in class, keep your directions simple. SAY them, loudly and distinctly, not at one hundred miles per hour (for the auditory learner) and WRITE them, PRINT THEM clearly on the board (for the visual learner.) You may find an occasional student who has difficulty with cursive writing but most can read it. Be organized in your directions. It will help him immensely.

If you've already prepared, or are planning to use, ditto sheets be sure that they have come out legibly printed or typed. Your disabled student will also breath a sigh of relief and offer psalms of Thanksgiving if you leave the reverse side blank. "Show through" is another hazard for him, further complicating an already difficult exercise. It can also throw off his delicate coping mechanism, a coping mechanism he may only be just starting to develop and of which he may still be a bit distrustful.

It is also well to bear in mind, at this stage, that students who can read printed material can not always also read cursive. Therefore, if possible, on Day One especially, remember to print. If ditto hand-outs are a part of the agenda, try to arrange to have them typed. Also, don't overwhelm him in the beginning with too much writing, too much reading, or too much copying from either the board or book or workbook. Build in variety in order to give yourself some time to get to know him and his learning style. Don't give him an opportunity to turn off before you ever have a chance to get started.

With each defeat there is further loss of ego strength and he needs all the ego strength he can muster! Also, if the day has been particularly strenuous he may resort to "losing" his paper, or tearing it up, or resorting to some other kind of unacceptable behavior in his frustration thus putting you in the situation of having to "do something." He may also be trying to preserve what ego strength he has by doing his best to have you throw him out of class, so that he can justifiably avoid work and thus save face. Try to prevent the dis-service to him of allowing him to lose control. He doesn't want it to happen any more than you do. And don't destroy him before he has a chance to show you where his strengths lie and what he can do.

Since anything written is usually considered disaster by the auditory learner, his tension will be reduced if you announce beforehand, before anyone even knows you have ditto hand-outs, that you (or the class) will read through it first, AFTER you have passed it out, and BEFORE anyone is to start to work on it. It is beneficial for the learning disabled student to have it in front of him and to follow along as you/the class read it aloud. Incidentally, this is particularly good for homework assignments as it provides him with the opportunity to ask questions before leaving your class if he still hasn't understood.

Your learning disabled student needs all the clues, cues, "for instances," "likes" and "as if's" that you can think of. He also needs your understanding. Perhaps most of all he needs your belief in him as a learner, as a learner among other student learners; in short, a student among students.

After all, he can learn, if you can provide the input in ways that can be picked up by his open channels, in other words, if you can turn on your creativity, ingenuity and originality and create different situations/modes for transmitting the information which you want him to pick up. The same holds true for output. Capitalize on his open channel and don't over-strain his areas of weakness. In essence, flexibility and a willingness to experiment are the keys here.

To help you to begin, some practical suggestions for variations in input and for student responses (output) are contained in the next chapter.

6

CLASSROOM STRATEGIES — GENERAL

Regardless of whether the student learns best through his auditory, visual or motor channel, all students with learning difficulties are more successful within a framework which encompasses the following characteristics. Actually, these strategies will help all of the students in your class.

— Minimize distractions, visual as well as aural.

— Set clearly defined limits: for classroom behavior
: for academic expectations (e.g. you must always have your pencil.)

— Keep your directions simple, preferably to not more than two or three steps. (e.g. Get out your math book, turn to page 24. When all students are on page 24 *then* proceed with your next directions.)

— If you have both aural and visual learners in your class try to present your directions both ways if possible. It will be a life-saver for your disabled student and repetition in different modes/channels will be helpful and reinforcing for all students.

— Seat him in the front of the classroom.

— Eye contact! It is important that he watch you, plus the fringe benefit for you of knowing that you have his attention. If he can't get the proper order of things (sequence) by *watching* you then be sure he *hears* you, looking right at you, eyeball-to-eyeball.

— Try to keep your voice at a comfortable classroom level and be sure to speak distinctly. Everyone has bad days but it is much more difficult for your students to understand teachers who are apt to shout. Also it makes them nervous and, for middle school students, often increases any subliminal awkwardness, should it exist.

— Be consistent. If you demand that the child always have his name and date in the upper right-hand corner of his paper, don't become careless on Friday and forget.

— Be firm. And be fair.

— Keep him on task.

— Be calm. Avoid threats and punishments with this population. Remember, for them being in school itself is trauma enough. The fact that they come at all is to their credit and to the credit of their families and former teachers.

— Provide a starting point that leads to immediate success. (Remember, he is convinced that he is stupid.) Don't worry that it might be too easy, you have plenty of time to correct for this later. Better to err on the easy side now than to turn him off at the outset.

— Provide enough time.

— Keep assignments short. (e.g. for him one paragraph instead of one page, three sentences instead of ten, three math problems instead of ten.)

— Arrange for him to work with another student who can "translate" your directions, with whom he can "read along," etc. This will work in math as well as other classes.

— Provide constant reassurance.

— Provide positive and immediate reinforcement. A nod or a smile will go a long way. Beware of saying "It's good." if it isn't, or "excellent" when it is only fair. Remember that the disabled student is not stupid and he will know if/when you are putting him on. He will not be fooled, and the tragedy is that not only will he begin to distrust you but it will also reconvince him that he really is stupid.

— Praise that part that is good. Even though the sentence

structure and/or spelling may be poor, the ideas may be good and/or the information valid.

— Be flexible with output. You can have your students (any of them) write, talk, read aloud, act it out, put it on tape, do an interview, create a skit/play, gesture, etc. Adjust the length of the assignment.

— Encourage extra credit assignments that are geared to his best learning channel.

— HOMEWORK: Do not exempt these students from homework. Instead, be flexible. Adjust the assignment to their learning modality and, if necessary, also adjust its length. Better to have one page learned or one concept firmly in place than a confused maze.

— Remember that he will probably need more review and reinforcement of learned material than the other students.

— Grade according to individual performance and progress rather than as measured against a pre-established norm for the entire class. In other words, a grade based on *his* performance, *his* assignments, *his* extra credit work, etc. Build flexibility into the *tool* which you use for measuring. Bear in mind that not all students respond at the same rate to the same measuring device.

— Emphasize his ability, not his disability. Work toward his strengths.

— Make it clear constantly that you know that he is not stupid.

— Make clear to him your flexibility and your enthusiasm for going along with him in any new learning techniques/schemes that he can dream up. Talk with his Special Needs teacher or tutor for ideas along these lines.

— Build up his self-esteem through seeing to it that he experiences success.

— Provide moral support. Whatever he does and however he does it, it will represent real effort and will probably have taken him considerably longer to accomplish.

— Beware the "He isn't trying" trap. If you find your

thoughts running along these lines, bring yourself up short. Has he tried? Has he found that he can't? Has he thus given up? Was the assignment too far out of his modality? (If he's an auditory learner, was there too much to write or to read?) Did he have enough time to complete it? Did it appear to him so lengthy and arduous that he has given up without even trying? Shorten it. If it is "none of the above", haul out one of your "extra strength" pills and see if you can invent another way of teaching the same concept. This is not to say that there are times when, in truth, he isn't trying. When he truly does give up, try to find out why. He will be tremendously relieved.

— Recognize that the disabled learner may fall apart for no apparent reason and at a time when all seems to be going very well. Suddenly his behavior disintegrates. He may just turn off. This is typical with these students. Occasionally they will get all bent out of shape over some trifling thing, and become morose and discouraged. Should this happen in the midst of your class, avoid making an issue out of it right then. Instead, try to talk with the student after the class has been dismissed.

— Remember that how the student feels about himself is VITAL to his success in learning. The more successful he feels, the less chance there is of his acting out with unacceptable behaviors, thus the fewer problems with which you will have to cope.

— Be available to him, not every second but on a mutually agreed upon contractual arrangement. And be sure that he fully understands this agreement.

— Talk with him. It may surprise you but it is amazing what he can tell you about his learning. Specifically:
  1) He can tell you what he can and cannot do.
  2) He will give you many clues to the way in which he learns best.
  3) He will be quite forthright in letting you know what his gaps are and how he can best assimilate the information.

— Consider the use of contracts. This can be especially effective in math. Furthermore, it has the added advantage of making your disabled student no different than any other since *all* members of the class are on contracts. Your bright student may be on his tenth, most on their sixth or seventh, and your disabled learner still laboring over his third. He gets his materials, sits down, and works along just as do all of the other students.

Not all subject areas lend themselves to a year-long contract approach but do try to work it in for some aspect of your discipline, preferably at the start of the term. By so doing your disabled student can hold his head up and feel, and *be,* an equal member of the group. He will relax and demonstrate a willingness to learn. Thus, your first hurdle is passed.

— Structure your grading system so that the two lowest quizzes (or whatever) will not count. Be sure that your students know this. (For the exceptional student who gets 95's on all of them provide a bonus. For instance, consider it work for extra credit or some such device.)

In this connection, consider throwing out the first one or two quizzes of the year. This is especially important if your purpose in giving them was primarily diagnostic, to ascertain how much they retained from last year, or to get an idea of their familiarity with the subject.

— Remember, nothing succeeds like success. Be sure that he experiences some each day.

— YOUR STUDENT'S *TUTOR:* Keep the tutor tuned in to what is going on in the class. Feed the tutor information — copies of assignments, instructions for major projects, book reports, oral reports, etc. Drop off copies of these assignments in the tutor's mailbox. (It is difficult for tutors to keep in touch with individual teachers since they have many students from many different classes.)

Feeding information about what is going on in class to the tutor provides her with the opportunity to gear her learning strategies around your current subject matter.

Remember too that if your student needs untimed and/or oral tests that he can take these with his tutor (rather than your administering it to him separately or

29

during class when you are also trying to do twenty other things.)

Your learning disabled student needs your continuing sensitivity, support, caring and belief in him as a viable human being and a potential learner. Perhaps without realizing it, he also depends on your creating an atmosphere in your classroom that has built into it the necessary components in which he can function successfully, as well as guarantees that will not let him go out of control. For him it will be another fear allayed.

Be organized! Of all of the concrete components, this is probably the most important. Plan ahead. Know your subject matter and what you're going to do today. Have your materials ready. Have something ready for your disabled learner the minute he enters your classroom — handing out worksheets, returning homework assignments, etc.)

Your self-organization provides him with a secure environment and framework, unthreatening parameters in which he can progress from one task to the next, without external worries and distractions. In short, be ready for him. Plan, and execute, ahead of time.

CLASSROOM STRATEGIES — THE VISUAL LEARNER

The strategies mentioned in the foregoing section entitled General Strategies apply to the visual learner also. In addition, the strategies given below apply specifically to the visual learner. (The section which follows provides strategies for the auditory learner.)

In essence, the big thing to keep in mind for the visual learner, is that he learns by SEEING. Thus, visuals of any kind are a great asset for him. If he can SEE the Mississippi River on a map he is much more likely to remember it than if he is just told that it runs north and south, dividing the United States almost in half. The same with mathematical calculations, he needs to SEE, or to VISUALIZE, or even to RE-VISUALIZE. Some teachers find themselves more successful with these students if they pretend to themselves that the student is deaf. This seems a bit extreme but if it works for you, fine.

Now for the strategies themselves. From the foregoing, some of them should not come as a surprise.

— Directions need to be visual, to be written out on the chalkboard or on paper. Check to ascertain if he can read a) cursive, b) your handwriting and c) things on the board (as opposed to a piece of paper which he has in front of him.) If directions must be aural, have him

30

repeat them and/or write them down.

— Keep your cool. It will probably be necessary to repeat directions which have been given orally. Remember to be specific with your directions (your blue science book, your yellow social studies workbook.)

— Student responds best to and needs visual clues/cues.

— Provide as much visual stimulation as possible. (e.g. drawings, maps, charts, films, slides, printed matter, etc.)

— Student will respond better to filmstrips and films than to tapes. Your school library may be able to provide some, as well as your Public Library.

— Utilize demonstrations whenever possible as student learns best if he can see it.

— Illustrate visually what you are saying — by a drawing, one or two words written on the board, pictures, slides, etc.

— Keep visual cues in front of the student. Provide an outline for the class discussion, to help him to focus.

— Encourage him to "visualize" what he hears. Emphasize for him the importance of his creating a mental picture, in living color preferably, so that he will retain the information.

— Encourage him to "visualize" the situations given in his math problems if it is aural work, e.g. 2/3rds plus 1/2.

— Remember that he will not do well with aural directions, don't let his difficulty in comprehending these get your goat.

— ORAL WORK: If this is a "must" in your class, try to abbreviate your demands of him. Keep it short. Allow him to use one-concept phrases and short sentences. Do not demand a lengthy oral report from him.

Remember that he may be able to produce visually but that he quite likely will not be able to explain the procedure as he goes along. (e.g. he can fix your engine but he can't tell you how he does it.)

— Present the key points in the lesson at the beginning and summarize them again at the end.

- Encourage the student to write down assigned tasks with due dates.

- Write out for him new words, terms, etc. so that he can visualize them.

- If necessary, provide a glossary for him.

- Encourage him to outline, underline, and use multi-colored pen for difference in emphasis.

- Suggest the use of acronyms to help him to revisualize and recall.

- For factual material, have him prepare flash cards, or make a game. Possibly a teacher aide or honor student can help in the construction of these.

- NOTE-TAKING: If he also has trouble with handwriting this will be a difficult task for him. Allow him to tape your lectures and transcribe them as homework. If written work is a MUST, abbreviate your assignment for him. Encourage him to use a typewriter.

  To encourage him to learn to take notes, have a scribe (a good student) take notes in duplicate (using carbon paper) that he can use to check his own notes, and thus teach himself to take notes.

- Oral reports: Permit (encourage?) the use of notes and/or other visual aids. If he finds it difficult to speak, do not hurry him.

- Remember to keep your rate-of-presentation reasonable. Just because you are a bit behind in your syllabus, don't take off at eighty miles per hour. You'll lose him entirely.

- Remember that because he is a visual learner does not mean that he is always adept at ALL things visual. He may be fine at reading and writing but awful with maps, pictures, charts and graphs, or any combination of these and vice-versa.

- TESTS/QUIZZES/EXAMS: Provide him with a written list/outline of the main points to be covered prior to the test and instruct him to think about these beforehand. This is particularly effective prior to an oral quiz or class discussion.

- Be flexible in the forms of your assignments and tests. Consider a drawing, montage, model, photographic essay, diagram, etc. as well as the conventional true/false, fill-ins and multiple choice questions.

- Consider giving him an un-timed test.

- Try to avoid crossing modalities for input and output, especially for exams and quizzes.

One final caution — bear in mind that whereas he learns best visually, it does not necessarily follow that he reads easily or well. Reading is just one of the forms which visual input can take (others would be maps, charts, acting, movies, TV, observing others, doing it himself, etc.) This is not to say that visual learners can not read, many can. It is simply to alert you.

In short, the visual learner must be able to see what it is that he is learning, either literally or in his mind's eye. Encourage this in every way possible. Help him to keep himself on track with this habit.

If his auditory weakness is his only disability he should be quite a successful learner.

CLASSROOM STRATEGIES — THE AUDITORY LEARNER

The strategies mentioned in the earlier section entitled General Strategies apply to the auditory learner also. In addition, the strategies given below apply specifically to the auditory learner. (The preceding section provided strategies for the visual learner.)

In essence, the big thing to keep in mind for the auditory learner is that he learns by HEARING. Thus, any auditory cues/clues are a great asset for him. He needs to HEAR about the Battle of Bunker Hill in order to remember it, as just reading about it may be too difficult and, in any event, holds little meaning for him. He needs to SAY everything in order to AUDITORIZE or hear it. He needs to AUDITORIZE for himself in order to make it stick. Don't be alarmed if he moves his lips while he's reading, it's one of his coping mechanisms. Some teachers find themselves more successful with these students if they pretend to themselves that they are blind. This seems a bit extreme but if it works for you, go to it.

Now for the strategies themselves. From the foregoing some of them should not come as a surprise to you.

- Remember that his comprehension will be better with oral presentations than visual.

- Discussions will be extremely beneficial for him.

33

— Permit him to discuss the material with other students, small groups.

— Be sure that he can see you when you are talking — giving directions, lecturing, etc.

— His comprehension may be better with oral reading rather than silent reading. Thus, let him take the book home to read it for homework, with a listener.

— Provide as much opportunity as possible for him to absorb information orally.

— Encourage the use of tapes, cassettes, records (your school and local library.) Utilize teacher aides and/or volunteers or other students to put material/assignments on tape or cassettes. Other students could do this during study halls. Or allow them to do it for extra credit. Let him take the book home so that his parents or friends or siblings can put it on tape.

— If reading is mandatory, try to keep it short.

— Remember to keep calm when he keeps losing his place in the text.

— Try to take the time to saunter over in his vicinity to be sure that he is working on the right page.

— If he also has difficulty writing, which he probably will, reduce the length of the assignment. Keep it short.

— Emphasize the importance for him of "hearing it," of saying it to himself, to a friend, or talking about it later at home. Encourage his family, including siblings, to read aloud to him — with the understanding that he is to "say it back" as they go along.

— Because of his good oral skills, encourage his participation in class discussions.

— DITTO MASTERS: The first rule is to be sure that they are clearly inked!
Since the auditory learner is probably not the best reader in the world, either type these or print them. The chances are that he can handle printed words more easily than cursive writing. (The Business students in your school can obtain good practice preparing these for you — or an aide if there is one about, a senior

citizen?)

Keep the vocabulary simple.

— Provide auditory clues/cues as much as possible.

— Be prepared for his having difficulty taking notes, copying from the chalkboard, writing definitions, etc. Patience. He will probably benefit from an outline — he can say it to himself, and it will help him to focus.

— TAKING NOTES: Encourage his taping your lectures and taking notes from his tape. He can stop and start the tape whereas such stopping and starting is not possible as you lecture.

— His spelling may not be good. Thus beware of creating a situation in which he receives an F in your subject because of spelling. (His spelling will probably make sense if you read it out loud.) Consider giving separate grades for content and spelling. After all spelling and/ or writing does not mean a poor grasp of the material.

— ASSIGNMENTS: Provide a written outline. Again, his friends and/or family can read this aloud to him for his internalization and execution.

— If writing is really arduous for him give him more time and/or reduce the length of the assignment. Consider also the possibility of fulfilling the assignment in a different way. For instance, via tape, collage, movie, film, project, pictures, drawing, skit, play, etc. Perhaps it could be a small group effort.

— REPORTS: Consider allowing him to dictate it to a friend who can then type it for him with spelling, etc. corrected. This is perfectly valid if it is the information/ synthesis that you are after.

— Encourage the use of acronyms, rhymes, songs and cheers or chants for ways of internalizing information. He can then sing this back to himself. (Many students learn their multiplication tables this way.) Thus poems or rhymes (about historical figures, mathematical progressions, characters in a story, main ideas, etc.) may be helpful for these students. Nonsense words can also be helpful.

— Remember not to go into orbit if you see his lips moving

while he is writing. He is saying it to himself in order to be able to get it on paper.

— Encourage him to learn to typewrite. He can then "talk" his book report or paper into the typewriter.

— Try to avoid crossing modalities — especially with exams.

— TESTS/QUIZZES/EXAMS: Be inventive. Will you settle for a telephone interview put on tape, a CB transmittal, an oral report, a drama, play, skit, TV script; posters, montages? If it must be written then it will be helpful for your student if you include some multiple choice, true/false, matching and short answer questions. Maybe when it comes to the essay he can do his on cassette in the library, or other quiet place.

Consider having someone read the questions to him, then he can put his answers on tape.

Better still, and depending on the grade level, give oral tests whenever you can (aides, honor students?)

Or, put his test on a cassette and leave a blank space for him to talk in his answer. If you want to save the cassette, provide him with an answer sheet.

— Consider the un-timed test.

One final caution — bear in mind that whereas he learns best through his auditory channel it does not necessarily follow that he can repeat everything right back to you. He can listen and understand, but he may have trouble repeating it for you. In a similar vein, a student may be able to repeat it for you beautifully, but he hasn't internalized very much. In short, because he learns best auditorially it does not necessarily follow that his verbal skills function with equal facility.

Tradition has it that learning comes from books, from the printed page. However, this is "book l'arnin' " and has only been possible on a large scale since the invention of the printing press and movable type. When you think about it, that's relatively recent.

Thus, it is important to remember that there is a much longer and highly respected tradition of oral history that goes back many hundreds of years through many cultures and throughout all of the world. The traditions, legends and cultures have been transmitted and kept alive by word of mouth. It is just as valid as the written word.

In today's society, where the oral/aural media boasts such vast audiences, and where communication media themselves are rapidly becoming more and more sophisticated, honor your auditory learner.

CLASSROOM STRATEGIES — PROCESSING

The strategies mentioned in the foregoing section entitled General Strategies will also help the student who has difficulty processing. With luck he does not also have any short-circuits with either his auditory or visual channels.

— Keep him focused on task.

— Be sure that your presentations are organized in sequential order.

— If keeping his place on the page is a problem, permit the use of a ruler or blank piece of paper which will aid him to proceed in the proper order. This would also apply to quiz/exam taking.

— If he learns best by doing, by hands-on activities, turn on your creative self and invent something. Better still, ask him for ideas.

— If he has difficulty retrieving information when asked (written or oral) yet can remember in a "doing" situation, try to build on this. Again, can he come up with an idea that is related?

— If he processes information more slowly than you'd like can you slow down? Are you going too fast for other members of the class as well? Are they losing something because of the non-stop, Express train rate of input delivery.

Speak clearly, distinctly and try to keep the vocabulary simple.

— Allow him to xerox someone else's notes.

— If writing is arduous for him:

  — reduce the length of the assignments
  — allow him more time
  — consider allowing him to rough-draft or dictate his report to a friend who can then type it for him. This is perfectly legitimate where internalization of material is your goal.

— Be conscious of how much copying you require, from board and/or from worksheets or workbooks. The same goes for note taking as mentioned above. Can your unfacile writer keep up? Will his energies go to "getting it down" rather than trying to assimilate it? Are you steering him toward a sacrifice of the forest for the tree?

Try to adjust for him, emphasize the highlights, the most important points, and thereby reduce the strain.

— Not all students benefit from assignments being written on the board. Sometimes they cannot read cursive, only printing. Sometimes reading anything on the board is such a strain that if there is a *lot,* they will decide it is too much and not even attempt to do it. Thus, try to keep it to small batches each day, rather than leaping from whole boards full on some days to none at all on others.

— If he can't write it, can he tell it to you? Utilize classroom aides, volunteers, honor society students, tapes, etc. And be sure to let him tell you at his own rate of speed.

— Consider using an un-timed test.

— If his difficulty is recall, are you willing to create and/or use tests with context clues? In other words, instead of requiring three long essays, how about one essay and some True/False, matching, fill-ins from a list provided, and multiple choice. The latter are particularly helpful for students with memory problems.

Again, this is perfectly ethical. After all, is it equitable always to test in the same modality? Switching from written to oral may shake up your visual learners but certainly, in the long run, it is fairer to all members of the class. After all, the point is not who writes more easily or talks more glibly but rather who understands the material which is covered by the test.

— Math: If the multiplication tables have not yet been learned, allow the use of a calculator or multiplication table. Make sure that the steps necessary to solve the problem are thoroughly understood in their proper sequence. Leave the memory to the machine or the multiplication table.

Or, if he has a method that works for him encourage him to use it (even if this is counting on his fingers. Orientals have for centuries and still do, sometimes in concert with the abacus.)

— If he learns concretely and is not yet able to abstract:

Be thankful that he recognizes that cars, motorcycles, buses, railroad trains and airplanes all have wheels even though he may not be able to abstract that they are all methods of transportation. Give him credit for the output which he is able to give rather than a zero because it wasn't the answer you have on your correcting sheet.

For the **Distractable learner:**

— Visual Distractability: He *sees* everything! Therefore:

- — Keep eye contact.

- — Seat him up front, with nothing in front of him and preferably where he does not see out the window or the door into the hall.

- — Seat him near quiet, non-leg/hand twitching students who will not disturb his peripheral vision.

- — See that he does not become transfixed by your necklaces, belt buckles, bracelets and/or other ornaments.

— Auditory Distractability: He *hears* everything! Therefore:

- — Minimize background noise — of other students, in corridors, of projectors, of your jewelry clanking and bangling, etc.

- — If possible and you have the opportunity, have him use headphones for instructions, listening, etc. This also blanks out surrounding noise.

For the Disorganized Learner:

This is the student who will drive you wild. His disability is that he literally is unable to organize himself. Further, because he appears knowledgeable his disorganization looks like carelessness, not-caring-ness, and a host of other irresponsible behaviors.

— Insist that he have a notebook and see to it that he writes down each and every assignment in it, within the "due date" box for the day on which it is due. This calendar should go for a month, so that he eventually develops the habit to plan ahead.

In addition to classroom assignments the calendar should also include holidays, concerts, field trips, and whatever else is a part of his life, so that he learns to take these things into consideration.

You may find it easier to have one big calendar in the front of the room. By so doing the disorganized student can copy it, and students who were absent yesterday can also check, for any additions and/or changes.

Another characteristic of the disorganized student is that he is extremely forgetful. Hold him to his calendar. You might even have him head it up with the materials which he must have in hand in order to gain entrance into your class (e.g. pencil, notebook, textbook or whatever.)

The crux with the disorganized learner is to make sure that he is provided with enough clues/cues to keep him on task. In other words, to prevent access to his ever-present Pandora's box of distractable items.

CLASSROOM STRATEGIES — SUMMARY

Working with learning disabled students does not require three years internship and a PhD. It can be done very simply. It takes a willingness to be flexible, a sincere effort to internalize his learning style, and a conscious effort to try to teach to that learning style, and, finally, a willingness to accept assignments (output) in alternative and/or abbreviated forms. As was pointed out earlier, you have had these students before. They are not unique to your classroom.

They may try your patience, their non-speedy progress may be discouraging to you from time to time, and, because school has been such a horror for them, they may be difficult to motivate sometimes. However, hang in.

— Be attuned

— Be sensitive to the student

— Believe in him as a learner

— Create an atmosphere in which he feels good about himself, as a person and as a learner.

— Accentuate the positive

40

— Avoid sarcasm; he will probably misunderstand it

— Build success into your everyday classroom demands

— Be flexible

— Be consistent

— Be caring

Actually, the above and the foregoing strategies, the untimed test and the oral report, are just two techniques of "individualizing" instruction. Individualizing instruction does not mean that you have to write out an entire course of study for each student. It can mean that, of course. However, most administrators recognize that that is an unrealistic expectation and burden for the teacher with five classes a day and one hundred and fifty students. Remember, some individualized adjustment for your presentations has always been necessary and has always been a part of your teaching style. Again, you've done this before.

The "individualized instruction" that gets bandied about so much these days is in the "how" — in the extent of your flexibility and imagination for "teaching" the student and in assessing the student for the success of your efforts. Your "input" is measured against his "output." He receives the grade at the end of the marking period but perhaps you should have one too. Anyone can be a purveyor of information; anyone can administer and grade tests. However, only a real Teacher can infuse/imbue knowledge, particularly over hurdles and around road blocks.

What is needed is the courage to try.

Avail yourself of Teacher Aides in your school, of volunteers, senior citizens, of students in the Honor Societies. Use them to type your dittos (your business course students?), make the tapes, listen to the oral exam/ quiz taker. Use them to draw up the calendar for the month, to research the visuals, find the auditory materials (at your local library?) etc., etc., etc.

Do not be overwhelmed.

Do not try to memorize and incorporate all of the foregoing strategies in one fell swoop. Remember, you are doing a number of these things already.

Proceed gradually. Pick out one or two strategies and try them out. Start with the General Strategies. Don't be disappointed if they don't work on the very first try. After all, were you able to ride a bicycle or ice skate after only one lesson? Give yourself time. Remember, Rome wasn't built in a day.

When you feel at ease with the first one or two strategies and find that they are coming fairly naturally, proceed to another. In between, consult with your student's Special Needs teacher or tutor. Perhaps there is a priority for your particular student or a recently discovered break-through regarding his learning style. The Special Needs teacher or tutor, who works with him in a small group situation, is in an excellent position to pass this on to you. Furthermore, this can be even more helpful if you have more than one learning disabled student in your classroom.

It won't take long before you realize that you have quite an extensive repertoire. As with everything else, the hardest part is in the beginning, in the ability to switch gears and to add another dimension to your teaching expertise.

Remember to utilize your student's tutor. This is extremely important. Keep the tutor informed regarding what is going on in class. Leave copies of assignments in her mailbox (projects due, book reports, oral reports, science projects, etc.) In this way, the tutor has the opportunity to gear her learning strategies around your current subject matter. It also provides a mutual point of discussion regarding how the student is achieving and progressing.

Finally, it may be necessary to remind your colleagues that the purpose of schools is for the education and edification of the students. Thus, in order to discharge their responsibilities as teachers, it is implicit that they seek out differences in learning styles so that they may adjust their teaching accordingly. Regrettably, some teachers have lost sight of this and have come to persuade themselves that it is the *student* who must adjust, both to their teaching style (sometimes rigid) as well as to their personalities (sometimes unyielding). It may also be necessary to remind them that the students whom they meet in their classrooms are teachable.

Over the years a great deal has been written about the purpose and function of the American public school. However, *nowhere* has it been stated that the schools exist for the convenience of the teachers. Remember that the student should and must come first.

If people will take the time to become familiar with a student's learning style and be willing to be flexible, it is surprising how quickly they forget that he is any different from any other student. Find ways to make him feel good about himself and you'll be embarrassed at how hard he will work for you. In fact, you'll be surprised when you're suddenly struck by the fact that you've had students like him before, that he is smart, and that "he isn't *that* different." What is different is that today he comes to you labeled. He comes to you preceded by a multitude of forms and formalities. Don't hold it against him. He'd be the first to apologize for the inconvenience.

7

THE NEW FEDERAL LEGISLATION — HOW IT HELPS *YOU*

Federal legislation (PL 94-142) for children with Special Needs is effective as of September, 1978. Bear in mind that it is modeled after Massachusetts Chapter 766, which has already been in effect since September of 1974.

Thus, if you are a teacher in Massachusetts, the legislation for students with learning difficulties is already in operation and has been for some years.

Therefore, your disabled student is currently, or has been, on an "Educational Plan." Thus, you have some valuable first-hand information right at your fingertips. You don't even have to read through the entire record if you don't have the time right now. Just look at the following items. They will give you a quick picture of your student, including the strategies under which he works the best and those that are apt to be the least successful.

The few minutes spent checking these over will pay big dividends. First, your student will be a familiar person to you when he arrives. Also, you will win him over at once because you are now in a position to spare him the humiliations that haunt him as he begins another school year. He dreads more of the inevitable failures as the days go by and each teacher essays, through trial and error — his errors, be it remembered — to discover how best he learns.

Thus, in being able to meet and greet him through his strengths you will not only have a friend for life but also you'll be a long way toward eliminating any propensity of his to disrupt your class.

1. **From the Educational Plan**
    a. Look at the "Learning Style". With this firmly in mind you should be able to reach your student with your material.

    b. Look at the General Objectives and the Specific Objectives. The latter will give you a good clue as to where your student is, in terms of current achievement as well as where the Team expects he will be when this current Plan expires.

c. Note the members of the Team that drew up this Plan. They are listed by name and relationship to the student. Thus, it is a simple matter to ascertain the teacher whom he had last year in your subject area. Don't hesitate to give that teacher a call. Probably she can give you some useful tips regarding your student, tips that may not show up within the Learning Style section and that possibly she didn't think to include when writing her own Assessment.

2. Teacher Assessments:

Of course you will want to read over the Assessment made by his last year's teacher. (The teacher's name is on the Assessment form together with the area taught.) However, it is a good idea to take another few minutes and read over the Assessments of the student's other teachers too. In this way you will get a more rounded picture; you will discover an area(s) in which he does well (shop, physical education, art, etc.)

3. Assessment by Special Needs Teacher:

Finally, give a look at the Assessment written by his last year's Special Needs teacher or tutor. Quite possibly you may pick up another clue or two on his learning style.

4. Special Needs Testing:

In connection with the foregoing, and to pull the whole thing together, you will find it extremely advantageous to look over his most recent testing results. Here you will find the real chapter and verse. This is not, repeat not, just a copy of school-wide SAT testing but rather an in-depth assessment of your student. You will be familiar with some of the tests, but most teachers are not familiar with all, particularly if the testing was done by a person trained in learning disabilities. To repeat, most teachers are NOT familiar with all of these tests. Thus, you are now provided with a beautiful excuse to seek out your student's current Special Needs teacher or tutor. Actually you don't even need an excuse; the fact that you are both working with this student is reason enough. But do seek out the Special Needs

Teacher or tutor. She can be most helpful in amplifying and/or giving you "for instances" regarding learning styles, as well as test interpretation. Also you will find it extremely helpful to be in touch with the Special Needs teacher or tutor as the year progresses.

If you want to get a jump on this, or feel that you'd like to bandy these terms about knowledgeably, a glossary is included at the back of the book.

As stated at the beginning of this chapter, the Massachusetts statute for children with Special Needs is already in effect. The Federal statute is mandated to go into effect in September of 1978. Since reports indicate that the Federal law is based in large part on the Massachusetts model the components mentioned above will also undoubtedly be incorporated. An individualized educational plan (IEP) is mandated, which is to contain educational goals and objectives. It is also stipulated that the student's teachers participate in its formulation. Thus, in all likelihood, the information will be available for you.

8

THE NEW FEDERAL LEGISLATION — NOT TO PANIC

As stated in the preceding chapter, PL 94-142, effective as of September, 1978, is based in large part on the Massachusetts model for children with "special needs," Chapter 766.

Although "mainstreaming" is an important element in both statutes it does *not* mean that all handicapped children are suddenly going to appear in your classroom.

What is important in the legislation are the terms "appropriate" and "least restrictive environment." The intent is to have the disabled student learning with his peers as much as possible, where this is "appropriate." Thus, "appropriate" placement for a student with Downs Syndrome (poor coordination, minimal expressive skills, marginal cognitive ability, etc.) should not be in your sophomore English class. For that student the "least restrictive environment" might very well be a small group, self-contained classroom for most of the school day. Pretty restrictive. However, that student might also be able to benefit from joining a regular eighth grade music class. Hence it might also be "appropriate" for that student to join that class for part of the school week. If this is the case a music class will be indicated in the individual educational plan beside the appropriate objective.

On the other hand, it might be highly "appropriate" for the learning disabled student to be in your English class and in other regular classes as well. He will benefit in many ways by being there. Specifically, interaction with his peer group will improve his ability to learn in class both from them and by being with them for classroom work. This is where learning style comes in. He can learn in your classroom, providing you are willing to be flexible and adjust your presentations, where necessary, to his learning style, to his best receptive process.

In addition to the learning disabled student attending "regular classes," it may also be "appropriate" for him to spend some time during the week with a tutor, to reinforce his learning disability coping mechanisms and/or skills. Thus, if everyone working with this student feels that this is "appropriate," it too will be incorporated into his individual educational plan.

In summary, not ALL disabled students will be "mainstreamed." Remember that the IEP's are generated by a team and that this team is made up of people — *teachers* — who have just recently or are currently working with this child. (Educational Plans must be reviewed and re-evaluated every school year.) Thus, the students whom you receive are not there by administrative edict. They are there because it is "appropriate." They are capable of learning. They are teachable.

Again, if you will take the time to familiarize yourself with their learning styles and be willing to be flexible in your approach and in your demands on them, you will be surprised at how quickly you will forget that they are different from your other students.

Don't panic about mainstreaming. Trust your colleagues.

GLOSSARY

GLOSSARY

Introduction

A glossary is a little bit like a dictionary, if you don't know where to start it makes it harder to look up the word. Thus, in order for this glossary to be as helpful as possible, it has been heavily cross-referenced. For instance, "discrimination" appears in three places, under "auditory discrimination," "visual discrimination" and "discrimination" itself. Under the latter, visual and auditory discrimination appear as sub-entries.

However, before getting into specific entries there are certain overall clues to the terminology, certain generalizations that are constant. A working knowledge of these is recommended since, together, they unlock the "code" to seventy-five percent of the terminology.

Overall Clues to Terminology

Prefix "a": Indicates without, not any, a negative

A = an absence of

As in asexual, asymmetric, amnesia

Prefix "dys": Indicates faulty, difficult, a deficiency

Dys = a difficulty with, a deficit

As in dyslexia (difficulty with reading), dysgraphia

(difficulty with writing).

The following terms appear almost always in tandem, being preceded in most instances by either "auditory" or "visual" (For example: "visual discrimination", "auditory discrimination", "visual memory", etc.) Thus, instead of trying to learn each tandem-term, concentrate instead on its component parts. In most instances they are not that different from the context in which you know them already.

Bear in mind that what is implied is "the ability to". In other words, "the ability to" discriminate, "the ability to" perform closure, and so on.

Closure: The ability of being able to perform closing or completing. A rounding out, or filling in of missing components, an end, a completeness.

Emphasis in learning disabilities is on "the ability to" recognize the whole when certain parts are missing. For instance, in a sentence, either letters or words may be missing (visual closure) whereas auditory closure refers to spoken language.

Discrimination: No different than in every-day language. The ability to make a clear distinction, to differentiate, to distinguish between. For example, to differentiate between "b" and "d" (visual) or to distinguish between the call of a Phoebe (fee-BE!) and a Chicadee (feee-beee), (auditory).

Figure-ground: This sounds much more complicated than it is. Omit the hyphen and dissect.

"Ground" equals the place, the environment, in which the activity takes place as a classroom, living room, restaurant, etc. The background.

"Figure" equals the item or task that is to be done therein.

Figure-ground is the ability to concentrate on the item or task without being distracted by the "ground", the place in which the task is being performed.

Memory: Nothing complicated here at all, perfectly straightforward. Memory, in learning disability parlance, is no different than in any other context.

Memory is the ability to store and retrieve information on demand, the faculty of remembering. Visual memory is remembering what has been seen; auditory memory is remembering what has been heard.

Perception: "Per" indicates "through." Thus, perception is the direct acquaintance with anything that is received *through* the senses.

The perceptual skills also include discrimination, figure-ground, closure, and sequencing. Thus, perception is *awareness* of incoming information. It is the recognition of input and its association with past experience.

Processing: Closely allied to perception. The "ability to" for the successful functioning of the perceptual skills.

Processing implies action. Action as in an oil refinery, wherein the crude oil is acted upon, is "processed," changed, so that it is now possible to expand its uses.

Change and/or integration has been effected.

So too with information. Within the processing center the input is acted upon; is organized and formulated, sorted and integrated for desired storage and/or retrieval (output).

The processing center is the pivotal area. The stored and/or raw data is processed, is *organized* by the thinking skills, thus also expanding associations and effecting greater understandings, assimilations, and/or syntheses.

Abstract: The ability of being able to generalize, see relationships and/or conceptualize from specifics. Relates to learning style.

Acalculia: The inability to manipulate arithmetic symbols and to perform simple mathematical calculations.

Agitographia: A writing disability characterized by very rapid writing movements and the omission or distortion of letters, words or parts of words.

Agnosia: The inability to obtain information through one of the input channels or senses (auditory, visual or tactile-kinesthetic) even though the receiving organ itself is not impaired.

Agraphia: The inability to be able to write or to write legibly.

Alexia: The inability to be able to read either written or printed language.

Amnesia: The lack or loss of memory.

Amusia: The loss of the ability to comprehend or produce musical sounds.

Anomia: Difficulty in recalling words or the names of objects.

Aphasia: The inability to comprehend, manipulate, or express words in speech, writing, or signs even though the individual may know what he wants to say.

Apraxia: Difficulty with motor output, with performing

purposeful motor movements. Extreme clumsiness.

Asymbolia: The inability to use or understand symbols, such as those used in mathematics, music, chemistry, etc.

Ataxia: The inability to coordinate motor activity. The movements are jerky, balance is a problem, and sometimes there are also speech and writing problems.

Auding: The ability to respond to spoken language *as well as* being able to listen, hear, recognize and interpret.

Auditory Dyslexia: Difficulty translating speech into writing; difficulty distinguishing between certain sounds of speech accurately; difficulty establishing the sound of the word with its written equivalent.

Auditory: Through the ears! (See below, Auditory _____.)

    Auditory association: The ability to relate material presented orally (words and concepts) in a meaningful way.

    Auditory blending: The ability to recognize the sound of individual letters and to be able to put them together into a word.
(Example: M — A — N to MAN.)

    Auditory closure: The ability to complete the whole auditorially when some of the parts are missing, either within a spoken word or a sentence.

    Auditory discrimination: The ability to distinguish (to "discriminate") between sounds which are heard and which may be somewhat alike.

    Auditory figure-ground: The ability to be able to concentrate on the task at hand despite the presence of other sounds (voices, miscellaneous noises) within the same environment. (e.g. the classroom.)

    Auditory memory: The ability to remember and recall words, digits, and information received through the auditory channel. This also includes memory of meaning. (See Auditory sequential memory.)

Auditory perception: The ability to receive sounds accurately and to correctly interpret what is heard.

Auditory processing: The ability of being able *to act upon* information received auditorially in order to abstract, generalize, classify, integrate, etc.

Auditory reception: The ability to obtain meaning from material which is presented orally.

Auditory sequential memory: The ability to remember and to repeat correctly a sequence (a series) of symbols just heard.

Auditory-to-visual association: The ability to switch from the auditory channel to the visual channel, from learning through the ears to learning through the eyes. Included is the ability to relate sounds to symbols. (Example: Being able to correctly identify the sound of the letter "r" and/or its letter name to the written "r" *and* transfer this association to other situations such as the word on the ditto sheet, the chalkboard or workbook.)

Blends: The ability to combine two consonants into a sound in which each retains its distinctive sound. Usually comes up in connection with reading or spelling.

Body image: The awareness of one's own body, arms, legs, hands, feet, etc. together with an awareness of their position in space and their relationship to each other.

Bradyslexia: An extemely slow rate of reading, writing or spelling.

Brain damage: Any injury to or infection of the brain that has resulted in organic impairment which now inhibits or impedes the normal learning process. This may come about before, during or after birth, or as a result of disease, surgery or accident.

Cerebral dominance: The establishment of one side of the brain as dominant over the other. It is generally recognized that this must take place in order to establish left or right handedness in individuals.

Channels: The pathways through which input is transmitted. These can be auditory, visual, tactile-kinesthetic or any combinations of these.

Chronological age: The actual number of years that a person has lived. Usually referred to in years and months.

Circuits: The pathways, channels through which input is transmitted. These can be auditory, visual, tactile-kinesthetic or any combination of these.

Closure: The ability to recognize and complete the whole when parts are missing, both within individual words or sentences. Auditory closure refers to input received through the ears. Visual closure refers to input received through the eyes.

Cognition: To become acquainted with, to know. The process of knowing, knowledge and/or the capacity for knowledge. Both thinking and processing skills are involved. To recognize.

Compensating process: The use and further development where possible of alternative intact channels in order to compensate for the channel which is impaired.

Concept: An idea generalized from a group or series of ideas.

Conceptualize: The ability to form ideas, to process information and experiences into meaningful groupings, generalizations and/or universals. The ability to grasp, to become aware, to comprehend and to formulate ideas. (The "con" in conceptual means "with." Thus increasing learning *with,* a coming together.)

Conceptual disorders: A malfunction in the thinking process and/or the inability to formulate concepts.

Concrete: Thinking or dealing with an object or idea on a very literal level. The frame of reference is things that are meaningful to *him;* ideas and objects that are within *his* experiential orbit. (Thus, sarcasm may be meaningless, and idioms difficult to grasp.)

Context cues/clues: These are aids for students who have difficulty with recall. For example, a student may not be able to describe where France is located but he can point to it if you provide him with a map. He cannot summarize a story but if lead questions are provided he can usually provide correct responses.

Cross modality: The ability to switch from one modality/channel to another. (For example: The ability to switch from receiving input visually to delivering output auditorially, or vice-versa.)

Decoding: A receptive skill. Usually used in reference to reading as in "he has trouble decoding." meaning he has difficulty reading (visual decoding). Auditory decoding would be he has trouble understanding the spoken word. More generally, decoding applies to the assigning of meaning to input received through any of the senses. Appropriate output may be verbal or non-verbal.

Developmental imbalance: A disparity in the developmental patterns of intellectual skills.

Digraph: Two vowels or two consonants together that make a single speech sound. Usually comes up in connection with the teaching of reading or spelling.

Diphthong: Two vowels together that make a sliding sound. Usually comes up in connection with the teaching of reading or spelling.

Directionality: This relates to the two sides of the body (laterality) plus the vertical axis — how each relates to the other, their position in space and to other objects or points in space plus the ability to translate this meaningfully, (left, right, above, below, beside, etc.).

Discrimination: The ability to detect the differences and likenesses between and among various stimuli.

> **Auditory discrimination:** The ability to differentiate between like and unalike sounds.

> **Visual discrimination:** The ability to distinguish likenesses and differences among symbols.

Distractability: The inability to "tune out" extraneous stimuli, thus usually poor attention span and/or intermittent concentration on the task at hand. Inability to subdue this extraneous, irrelevant stimuli despite best intentions.

Dominance:

Cerebral dominance: The establishment of one side of the brain as dominant over the other. It is generally recognized that this must take place in order to establish left or right handedness in individuals.

Mixed dominance: The inclination to perform some activities with the right hand or foot and shifting to the other for other activities. For example, writing with the right hand but playing tennis with the left.

Dyscalcula: Difficulty in coping with mathematics. Difficulty with comprehending mathematics as well as understanding the relationships between mathematical symbols and concepts. Difficulty with calculations and number manipulation.

Dysfunction: The impaired functioning of _____ (whatever follows).

Dysgnosia: Difficulty in being able to remember which symbols represent which concepts, i.e. relationships of concept-symbol relationships.

Dysgraphia: Difficulty writing. This can be the actual physical (motor) process required for writing or the difficulty of being able to express ideas in writing, or of the symbols required for writing (mathematical as well as letter symbols).

Dyslexia: Difficulty with reading. When viewed through the criteria of academic success this is probably the most serious and debilitating learning disorder.
   The difficulty may take many forms, including seeing letters in their mirror image, reversals of letters, inability to distinguish the spaces between words, etc., etc.

Dysnomia: The situation in which the individual knows the word he is trying to say, recognizes it when someone else says it for him, but cannot recall it himself.

Dysphasia: Difficulty comprehending the spoken word and/or speaking, receptive and expressive dysphasia respectively.

Dyspraxia: Difficulty coordinating muscular activity.

Echolalia: Meaningless repetition of words, sounds or phrases. Also tendency to mutter while reading or writing.

Emotional blocking/overtones: The inability to make satisfactory progress due to over-riding anxieties. These anxieties may or may not be school related.

Emotional liability: Students with learning disabilities are prone to exhibit emotionalism from time to time for no apparent reason, including times when things are going well.

Encoding: An expressive skill. Usually used in reference to writing as in "He has difficulty encoding" meaning that he has difficulty writing (visual encoding). Auditory encoding would be he has difficulty speaking, i.e. verbal encoding.

More generally, encoding involves output that necessitates motor involvement, such as the muscles of speech (verbal), of the arm-hand (written), eye-hand (written), or "body language".

Endogenous: A condition or defect based on hereditary or genetic factors.

Etiology: The cause or reason for the condition.

Exogenous: A condition or defect resulting from other than hereditary or genetic factors.

Expressive language: The ability to communicate through speaking, writing or gesturing.

Eye-hand coordination: The ability of the hand and the eye to perform together without difficulty. This skill is necessary for copying from the chalkboard, for instance, or to take notes. It is also referred to as "perceptual motor match."

Feedback: That which is desired from the student by the teacher, in an academic situation.

Figure-ground: The ability to separate out from the background the task that is to be accomplished.

> **Auditory figure-ground:** The ability to "tone out" the background noises in order to concentrate on what is being said.

> **Visual figure-ground:** The ability to "tune out" the background sights (out the window, the student beside and in front of) in order to concentrate on paper or book or chalkboard.
>
> In short, the ability to separate out from the surrounding environment (ground) that on which one wishes to concentrate (figure).

Fine motor: The coordination necessary for writing. (As opposed to gross motor which would be jumping, skipping, etc.)

Gestalt: A term indicating an entity whose properties are more than just the sum of its parts.

Gnosia: The ability to know, of knowing.

Grammatic closure: The ability to automatically use correct grammar and syntax.

Gross motor: The ability to coordinate the larger muscles such as to successfully jump, skip, run, etc. (as opposed to fine motor which involves handwriting, etc.)

Hand-eye coordination: The ability of the hand and the eye to perform together without difficulty. In other words, to see *and* to write. Visual *and* motor coordination. Also referred to as perceptual-motor match. This skill is necessary in order to be able to copy from the chalkboard and/or to take notes.

Handedness: Refers to left or right handed preference of individuals.

Hemispherical dominance: See cerebral dominance.

Hyperactivity: The inability to remain still for any length of time. Constant activity of hands, head, legs, feet, arms, practically perpetual motion.

Hypoactivity: Activity that is less than normal, marked by extreme lassitude.

Impulsivity: Behavior characterized by acting before thinking, by being in the act of doing and possibly not even then being aware of consequences.

Inner language: The process of thinking utilized for the integration of input, academic as well as experiential, of making it one's own.

Kinesthetic: Pertaining to the muscles — doing. Thus, included is talking (the muscles of speech), writing (the muscles of the hand and arm), as well as body movement itself.

Language association: The ability to understand what is read (visual) or, spoken, the ability to associate the recognized word with its meaning in context. (Some students can read or say but cannot understand.)

Language classification: The ability to assign meaning to words by grouping likes and similarities.

Language formulation and syntax: The ability to organize words into meaningful phrases and sentences utilizing accepted grammatical rules.

Laterality: An awareness of left and right sidedness, as this pertains to the self as well as to one's position in space and/or other objects or people also occupying that space. See Dominance.

Lateral confusion: See Mixed Laterality.

Learning disabilities: One or more significant deficits affecting the essential learning processes of either perception, integration and/or expression (written or oral) or any combination of these. These deficits are diagnosed through accepted testing procedures and defined according to these procedures.

Students with learning disabilities frequently demonstrate discrepancies between expected and actual achievement. Areas most often affected are speaking, reading, writing, mathematics, and, less frequently, spatial orientation. Because of these difficulties IQ's are frequently depressed.

Learning style: The method, technique or modality through which the student learns the best. For some people this is through the eyes ("If I can *see* it, I remember it best."), for others through the ears ("If I can *hear* it, I remember it best."), and for others *doing* it. Thus visual, auditory and motor (or tactile-kinesthetic) channels or pathways for learning — different learning styles.

The learning disabled student may have one or sometimes more than one of these channels impaired, hence it is important to be aware of learning styles in order to provide input through the open or receiving channel.

Linguistic approach: A method of teaching reading using whole-word patterns. For instance, beginning with "an" and then adding "r", "t", "m" so that the student learns "ran", "tan", "man", etc. Often more successful with visual learners especially if they have a good sight vocabulary. (See Phonics for alternative method.)

Maturational lag: Slower development in some of the areas necessary for learning (physical, social-emotional and/or cognitive) where the student's intellectual functioning may be close to average, average or possibly even above average.

Memory: The ability to store and retrieve upon demand information previously obtained through experienced sensations and perceptions. In short, recall.

Auditory memory: The ability to recall that which has been received through the ears.

Visual memory: The ability to recall that which has been received through the eyes.

Mental age: The level of mental ability. Usually referred to in years and months.

Minimal brain dysfunction: A mild or minimal neurological abnormality that causes learning difficulties in children whose intelligence is otherwise near normal. It's use as an umbrella term is too simplistic.

Mirror image: The inclination to view things from right to left.

Mirror reading: The inclination to read words or numbers from right to left (backwards) as "saw" for "was" or 48 for 84.

Mixed dominance: See Mixed laterality.

Mixed laterality or lateral confusion: The tendency to perform some activities with the right hand or foot and some with the left. For instance, writing with the left hand but playing tennis with the right. A shifting from one side preference to the other.

Modality: The avenues, pathways, channels, circuits through which sensory impressions are transmitted to the brain and by which the student learns. For academic learning these consist primarily of the visual modality, the auditory modality and the motor, or tactile-kinesthetic, modality.

Modes of learning: In academic situations these are the visual mode, the auditory mode and the tactile-kinesthetic mode. See Modality above.

Motor: Motor is doing. It is involving the use of the muscles. Included are the muscles for speech and those for writing, as well as those for body movement. The term tactile-kinesthetic is often used instead of motor (tactile - touching, kinesthetic - doing).

> **Fine motor:** Refers to movement requiring a fairly high degree of muscle sophistication, e.g. writing.

> **Gross motor:** Refers to large body movements such as running, jumping, etc.

> **Visual motor:** Refers to the ability to coordinate the eye and the hand. This ability is necessary for copying from the chalkboard.

Multi-sensory approach: The utilization of as many modalities/chanels/pathways together for input, and again for desired output. The combining (or in-conjunction use) of visual, auditory and tactile-kinesthetic modes.

Non-language cues: In textbooks or by teacher and/or student — the use of color, underlining, indentions, capitalizing, arrows, asterisks, boxing (color or columns), etc. to emphasize, highlight and/or clarify material.

Students should be encouraged to develop what works best for them.

Oral aphasia: The inability to be able to say the intended word or to enunciate properly.

Pathways: The avenues or channels through which input is transmitted to the brain. See Modality.

Perception: Direct acquaintance with anything that is received through the senses.

The perceptual skills also encompass the areas of discrimination, figure-ground, closure, and sequencing. Thus perception is *awareness* of incoming information. It is the recognition of input and its association with past experiences.

Perceptual disorder: A dysfunction in the awareness of objects, relations, or qualities due to difficulty in interpreting input received through the senses.

Perceptual-motor: The *interaction* of motor activity with the various perceptual channels. Specifically, the interaction of motor with visual, auditory and tactile-kinesthetic. Laterality is also involved.

Perceptual-motor match: The *process* of collecting and arranging input form the motor system with input received from perceptual exploration. The process of comparing, collecting and collating input from these two areas. See also "hand-eye coordination."

Perceptually handicapped: A term applied to a student who has difficulty learning because of perceptual dysfunction(s). See Perception.

Perserveration: The tendency to continue an activity or an act long beyond the time for which it makes any sense to do so. This activity may or may not have been appropriate when it commenced. It may take place in any mode.

Phonics: A method of teaching reading in which the emphasis is placed on sound, one *sounds out* the letters. Often more successful with auditory learners. (See Linguistic approach for alternative method.)

Phonetics: Of, relating to, or consisting of speech sounds. (The phonetic guide in your dictionary.)

66

Processing: Closely allied to perception. The "ability to" for the successful functioning of the perceptual skills.

Action is required by the thinking skills for the organization of stored information and/or input for present or future desired output. The processing center is the pivotal area.

Psycholinguistics: Combines aspects of psychology and language in the consideration of the total field of language study. Emphasis is on what is meant by what is said.

Psychomotor: Refers to the effect on motor skills of and by the psychological processes. For instance, you walk without even thinking about it but are petrified to put one foot in front of the other when faced with a 6″ wide plank across a 50′ drop.

Reauditorization: The ability to recollect and retrieve what has been heard over long and short periods of time for spontaneous usage. In short, the retrieval of *auditory* images.

Receptive language: Language that is spoken or written and hence *received* by the student.

Retardation: Difficulty with the capacity to learn. No definite brain damage is indicated in the history or from neurological findings; nor is there any evidence/suggestion of other cause(s).

Reversals: This refers to transpositions of letters, numbers or sounds. Also included is the reversal of letters themselves, such as "m" for "w", etc.

Revisualization: The ability to retrieve what has been seen over long and short periods of time. In short, the retrieval of *visual* images.

Semantics: A term in linguistics referring to the meaning of words.

Semantic aphasia: The inability to comprehend word meaning despite the fact that the student may be able to pronounce or repeat or read them.

Sensory: That which is received by the senses. For academic learning these sensory pathways are visual, auditory and tactile-kinesthetic. In addition are the senses of smell and taste.

Sensorimotor: This term refers to input from the sensory channels and output through the motor channel. Thus, the motor channel reflects what is happening within a given sensory channel.

Sequencing: The ability to remember *in order* that which has been received through a sensory channel — through either the auditory, visual or tactile-kinesthetic channel or through a combination of these. (See also Auditory sequencing and Visual sequencing.)

Social perception: The ability of being able to be aware of one's social environment, of the needs of other people as well as of one's own.

Sound-symbol relationship: The ability to relate the sound of a letter or word with its written counterpart. (See Auditory blending.)

Spacial orientation: Refers to an awareness of self in space. This includes direction, position, distance and the judging thereof.

Spacial relations: Refers to the relationship in space of two or more objects. Also included is a change in position of those objects, such as rotation. "Objects" include people as well as things.

Substitution: The unconscious substitution of a letter or word for another either in reading or in writing (litter for letter, cat for cot). Also the inability to note minor details that distinguish details such as punctuation, asterisks, color bands, etc.

Symbolization: A synonym for language that is beginning to show up in the literature. For instance, "graphic symbolization" to mean writing. The fields of mathematics and music have always dealt in symbols.

Syndrome: A group or cluster of symptoms which characterize a specific behavior.

Tactile: This term refers to touching. See Tactile-kinesthetic.

Tactile-kinesthetic: A term frequently used synonymously with "motor." Tactile is touching, kinesthetic is doing. The tactile-kinesthetic channel is one of the main sensory channels for input.

Task analysis: The exercise of very carefully analyzing the elements required of a given task and the processes required for their performance. (Are you demanding more than your disabled learner's skills can deliver; or too much in his area of greatest weakness?)

Telescoping: Refers to the omission of parts of words in reading or spelling (tday for today, birthdy for birthday, etc.)

Verbal expression: The ability to express one's self by speaking.

<u>**Visual**</u>: Through the eyes! (See below, Visual _____ .)

    Visual acuity: Refers to the sharpness of vision.

    Visual agnosia: The inability to perceive the overall symbol (word, number, chart, map, etc.) and see instead only broken up portions.

    Visual aphasia: The inability to recognize printed words as indicative of the day-to-day speaking vocabulary. In other words, the inability to perceive that print is talk but in another form.

    Visual association: The ability to relate material presented visually (words, maps, charts, etc.) in a meaningful way.

    Visual closure: The ability to complete the whole visually when some of the parts are missing.

    Visual discrimination: The ability to distinguish (to "discriminate") between images that may be similar. For example, between "b" and "d", "w" and "m", etc. In addition to shapes this also includes sizes, shapes, position, color, horizontal and vertical, brightness, etc. (obviously numbers are also included.) The ability to recognize similarities and differences.

    Visual figure-ground: The ability to be able to concentrate on the task at hand despite the presence of other visual stimuli (flapping curtains, people moving, etc.) which are taking place simultaneously in the same environment.

Visual memory: The ability to remember and recall information received through the visual channel. This also includes memory of meaning.

Visual motor: The ability to relate visual stimulus with motor response. The most obvious example is that of writing. Also mathematics.

Visual motor coordination: For achievement and success in school this ability to coordinate *visual stimulus* with motor output is practically mandatory — for writing, for copying from the chalkboard, for note taking, and for quizzes and exams.

Visual perception: The ability to see something in all of its detail — not just its main features of sizes, shapes or colors. In other words, the ability to organize and interpret input received through the visual channel.

Visual processing: The ability of being able *to act upon* information received visually in order to form abstractions, generalize, classify, integrate, etc.

Visual reception/visual decoding: The ability to obtain meaning from what is seen (symbols — words and figures — pictures, graphs, charts and written words).

Visual sequential memory: The ability to remember and to repeat correctly a sequence (a series) of symbols just seen.

Visual-to-auditory association: The ability to switch from the visual channel to the auditory channel, from learning through the visual channel to learning through the auditory channel. Or input via the first and required output through the second.

Written expression: The ability to use words to express thoughts and/or ideas.